JOKES

FOR

7 YEAR

OLDS

FROM.....................

How did the sea greet the beach?

a. It waved!

Where do squids go when they feel sick?

a. To the doctorpus!

How do you fix a hole in a Jack-o'-Lantern?

a. With a pumpkin patch!

Where do cats keep their lipstick?

a. In their purrses.

How do pigs get to the hospital?

a. In the hambulance!

Why was Cinderella bad at basketball?

a. Because she ran from the ball!

What is a duck's favorite snack?

a. Cheese and quackers.

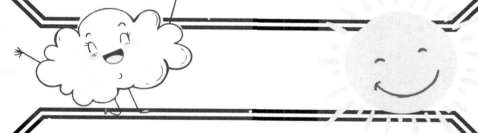

How do fish weigh themselves?

a. On scales!

How did the duck break the egg?

a. He quacked it!

Where do cows go on Friday night?

a. To the moovies.

Why did the fisherman get a telescope?

a. To look at starfish!

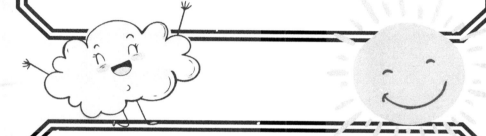

What do you call a pretty ghost?

a. Bootiful.

What game do barbers play at their birthday?

a. Musical hairs.

What do crabs eat for lunch?

a. Sandwiches.

Why did the teddy bear stop eating?

a. Because it was stuffed.

What did the snail use to call his mom?

a. His shell phone.

How do you let a bee inside your house?

a. You buzz it in.

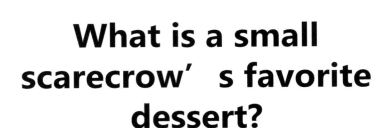

What is a small scarecrow's favorite dessert?

a. Strawberry short cake.

What did the banana say to his crush?

a. "I have peelings for you!"

What is a star's favorite day of the week?

a. Sunday.

What do cows celebrate at the beginning of the year?

a. Moo Year's Day!

What do you say to a bunny on its birthday?

a. "Hoppy birthday!"

What do you call an amazing omelet?

a. Eggcellent!

What does lightning wear under its clothes?

a. Thunderwear.

How do you wrap up a cloud?

a. With a rainbow!

What did the penguin say when it had enough?

a. "Snow more!"

What sport do you play with cereal?

a. Bowling.

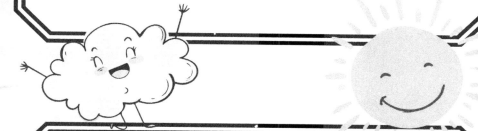

Why did the ostrich make the peacock a cake?

a. Because it was his birdday!

What do trees wear when they go swimming?

a. Their trunks!

Where do baseball players get clean?

a. In the bat tub!

What do snakes study in school?

a. Hisstory!

How do you keep a barbershop cool?

a. You use hair conditioning!

What is crunchy and looks for buried treasure?

a. A pirate chip!

What is a penguin's favorite kind of soup?

a. Chilly!

What do ghosts eat off a cone?

a. Ice scream.

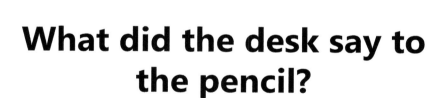

What did the desk say to the pencil?

a. Write on!

What is the best day of the week to eat potatoes?

a. Fryday!

What do you call a hurtful collar?

a. A pain in the neck!

Why was the vampire acting silly?

a. Because he was batty!

What was the pirate's two favorite letters?

a. Arrrrrrrrrrr and the C!

What do you tell a mouse when you take its picture?

a.   "Say cheese!"

What were the king and queen doing with the football?

a. They were throne it around!

What do you call a dancing sheep?

a. A baaallerina!

Why do grizzlies have cold toes?

a. Because they're always walking around bearfoot!

What do you call a firecracker that returns when you throw it?

a. A boomerang.

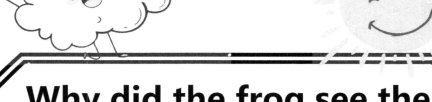

Why did the frog see the doctor?

a. It needed a hoperation.

What do insects call their mom's sister?

a. Antie!

What do brooms do when it's bedtime?

a. They go to sweep.

Why did the man put cheese and a trap next to the computer?

a. Because he wanted to catch a mouse!

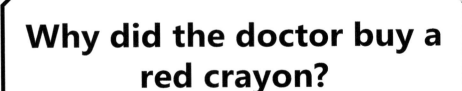

Why did the doctor buy a red crayon?

a. Because she needed to draw blood!

Which school supply is in charge of the whole classroom?

a. The ruler!

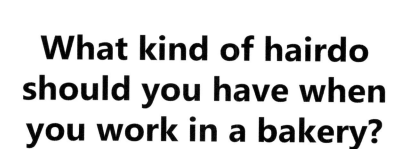

What kind of hairdo should you have when you work in a bakery?

a. A bun!

What is a Canadian's favorite dessert?

a. Chocolate moose.

What do lions sing at Christmas?

a. Jungle bells.

What do kittens climb?

a. Meowntains!

What do you call a pretty honey-maker?

a. Beeautiful!

What do birds say when they want candy?

a. Trick or tweet.

What do you call your mother in Egypt?

a. Mummy!

What do you do when a snake is under the mistletoe?

a. You give it a hiss!

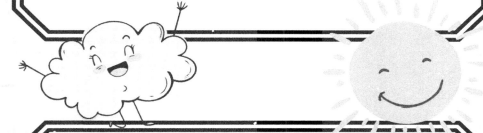

What fruit makes the best scarf?

a. Necktarines.

Why did Monday and Tuesday have to go to the gym?

a. Because they were weakdays.

What do sparrows call their girlfriends?

a.   "Tweety pie!"

What do old elves use to walk?

a. Candy canes.

Why should you never race a jungle cat?

a. Because they' re cheetahs!

What did the bike say to his crush?

a.   "I wheelie like you!"

What do Santa's helpers learn in Kindergarten?

a. The elfabet!

What do you say to make a tomato speed up?

a.   "Try to ketchup!"

What do call a vegetable that makes music?

a. A drumbeet.

What do you call a noodle on your leg?

a. Macaroknee.

What do you call a puppy in the desert?

a. A hotdog!

Why are calculators so dependable?

a. Because you can count on them!

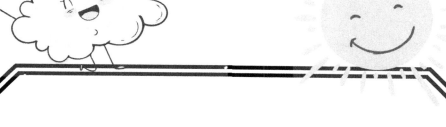

What do you call a lumberjack pig?

a. Pork chop!

What do ghosts call their fathers?

a. Deady!

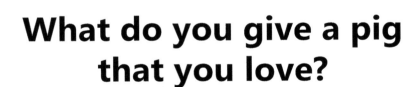

What do you give a pig that you love?

a. A hog and a kiss!

What is a bear without any ears called?

a. B.

Cars run on fuel, what do cheetahs run on?

a. The ground!

What do bats do with their friends?

a. They hang out.

Who stole all the bubbles from the bathtub?

a. A robber ducky!

What is a bear's favorite summer treat?

a. A pawpsicle.

How do bells propose?

a. With a ring!

What does a spider do on vacation?

a. It surfs the web.

What is a ghost's favorite pasta?

a. Spooketti.

How do giraffes greet each other?

a. They say, "High there!"

What letter hurts you if you bother it?

a. The letter B.

What do sharks need to stay healthy?

a. Vitamin sea.

What is the best time to fight a dragon?

a. At knight time.

What do heroes eat their soup out of?

a. Super Bowls!

What are the quietest animals on the farm?

a. Shhheep.

What chore did the man do in his sleep?

a. He mowed the yawn!

What bird gets arrested for stealing?

a. Robins!

How do lobsters get when they have to wake up early?

a. Crabby!

What do you say to your girlfriend on a volcano?

a. "I lava you!"

Why did the robin go to the library?

a. To look for bookworms!

What did the sheep say to his girlfriend on Valentine's Day?

a. "I love ewe!"

What powers your smoke detector and hangs upside-down?

a. Batteries!

What kinds of plates do aliens use?

a. Flying saucers!

Where does Cinderella go to meet polar bears?

a. To the snowball!

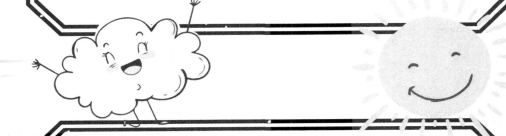

What did the cherry say to his girlfriend?

a. "I love you berry much!"

Why did the music teacher bring a ladder to class?

a. To get to the high notes!

Why did the fish turn in her math quiz?

a. Because she finished!

Printed in Great Britain
by Amazon

10429212R00032